TWO WAYS OF SEEING

TWO WAYS OF SEEING

An Anthology of Poems and Photographs

EDITED BY

WILSON G. PINNEY

College of San Mateo

PHOTOGRAPHS BY

ALLEN SAY

LITTLE, BROWN AND COMPANY BOSTON

FIRST PRINTING

Published simultaneously in Canada
by Little, Brown & Company (Canada) Limited

PRINTED IN THE UNITED STATES OF AMERICA

Acknowledgments

W. H. Auden, "The City." Copyright 1941 and renewed 1969 by W. H. Auden. Reprinted from W. H. Auden, *Collected Shorter Poems 1927–1957* (where it appears as "The Quest, V"), by permission of Random House, Inc., and Faber and Faber Ltd.

Arna Bontemps, "Southern Mansion." Copyright © 1963 by Arna Bontemps. Reprinted from *Personals*, 1963, by permission of Harold Ober Associates, Incorporated.

Leonard Cohen, "Suzanne." © 1966 by Project Seven Music, a division of C.T.M.P., Inc., New York, New York.

Hart Crane, "Chaplinesque." Copyright 1933, 1958, 1966 by Liveright Publishing Corporation. Reprinted from *Complete Poems and Selected Letters and Prose of Hart Crane*, by permission of Liveright, Publishers.

e. e. cummings, "from spiralling ecstatically this." © 1956 by E. E. Cummings. Reprinted from his volume, *95 Poems*, by permission of Harcourt, Brace & World, Inc.

Emily Dickinson, "I'm Nobody! Who Are You?" Reprinted by permission of the publishers and the Trustees of Amherst College from Thomas H. Johnson, Editor, *The Poems of Emily Dickinson*, Cambridge, Mass.: The Belknap Press of Harvard University Press, Copyright, 1951, 1955, by The President and Fellows of Harvard College.

Ray Durem, "Award." Copyright © 1964 by Langston Hughes. Reprinted from *New Negro Poets: U.S.A.*, by permission of Indiana University Press.

William Everson, "Fish-Eaters." Copyright 1939 by William Everson. Reprinted from William Everson, *The Residual Years*, by permission of New Directions Publishing Corporation.

Lawrence Ferlinghetti, "Constantly Risking Absurdity." Copyright © 1958 by Lawrence Ferlinghetti. Reprinted from Lawrence Ferlinghetti, *A Coney Island of the Mind*, by permission of New Directions Publishing Corporation.

Robert Frost, "The Road Not Taken." Copyright 1916, © 1969 by Holt, Rinehart and Winston, Inc. Copyright 1944 by Robert Frost. Reprinted from *The Poetry of Robert Frost*, edited by Edward Connery Lathem, by permission of Holt, Rinehart and Winston, Inc.

Allen Ginsberg, "The Wild Orphan." Copyright © 1956, 1959 by Allen Ginsberg. Reprinted from Allen Ginsberg, *Howl and Other Poems*, by permission of City Lights Books.

Robert Graves, "Spoils." Copyright © 1958 by Robert Graves. Reprinted from Robert Graves, *Collected Poems*, 1961, by permission of Collins-Knowlton-Wing, Inc.

Thomas Hardy, "Hap." Copyright 1925 by The Macmillan Company. Reprinted from *Collected Poems of Thomas Hardy*, by permission of The Macmillan Company; Thomas Hardy's Estate; Macmillan & Co. Ltd, London; and The Macmillan Company of Canada Ltd.

Gerard Manley Hopkins, "Pied Beauty." Reprinted from *Poems of Gerard Manley Hopkins*, edited by W. H. Gardner and N. H. Mackenzie, published by Oxford University Press, 1967.

A. E. Housman, "To an Athlete Dying Young." Copyright 1939, 1940, © 1959 by Holt, Rinehart and Winston, Inc. Copyright © 1967, 1968 by Robert E. Symons. Reprinted from "A Shropshire Lad"—Authorised Edition—from *The Collected Poems of A. E. Housman*, by permission of Holt, Rinehart and Winston, Inc.; the Society of Authors as the literary representative of the Estate of A. E. Housman; and Jonathan Cape Ltd, publishers of A. E. Housman's *Collected Poems*.

Randall Jarrell, "The Death of the Ball Turret Gunner." Copyright © 1945, 1969 by Mrs. Randall Jarrell. Reprinted from Randall Jarrell, *The Complete Poems*, by permission of Farrar, Straus & Giroux, Inc.

Robinson Jeffers, "The Deer Lay Down Their Bones." Copyright 1954 by Robinson Jeffers. Reprinted from Robinson Jeffers, *Selected Poems*, by permission of Random House, Inc.

Rudyard Kipling, "The Way Through the Woods." Copyright 1910 by Rudyard Kipling. Reprinted from *Rudyard Kipling's Verse: Definitive Edition*, by permission of Mrs. George Bambridge; Doubleday & Company, Inc.; and The Macmillan Company of Canada.

Robert Lowell, "Skunk Hour." Copyright © 1958 by Robert Lowell. Reprinted from Robert Lowell, *Life Studies*, by permission of Farrar, Straus & Giroux, Inc.

CONTENTS

vii

x

xi

xii

TWO WAYS OF SEEING

Henry Vaughan

Man

Weighing the stedfastness and state
Of some mean things which here below reside,
Where birds like watchful Clocks the noiseless date
    And Intercourse of times divide,
Where Bees at night get home and hive, and flowrs
      Early, aswel as late,
Rise with the Sun, and set in the same bowrs;

2

I would (said I) my God would give
The staidness of these things to man! for these
To his divine appointments ever cleave,
    And no new business breaks their peace;
The birds nor sow, nor reap, yet sup and dine,
      The flowres without clothes live,
Yet *Solomon* was never drest so fine.

3

Man hath stil either toyes, or Care,
He hath no root, nor to one place is ty'd,
But ever restless and Irregular
    About this Earth doth run and ride,
He knows he hath a home, but scarce knows where,
      He sayes it is so far
That he hath quite forgot how to go there.

4

He knocks at all doors, strays and roams,
Nay hath not so much wit as some stones have
Which in the darkest nights point to their homes,
    By some hid sense their Maker gave;

Man is the shuttle, to whose winding quest
        And passage through these looms
God order'd motion, but ordain'd no rest.

ALEXANDER POPE

Epistle II

Know then thyself, presume not God to scan;
The proper study of Mankind is Man.
Plac'd on this isthmus of a middle state,
A Being darkly wise, and rudely great:
With too much knowledge for the Sceptic side,
With too much weakness for the Stoic's pride,
He hangs between; in doubt to act, or rest;
In doubt to deem himself a God, or Beast;
In doubt his Mind or Body to prefer;
Born but to die, and reas'ning but to err;
Alike in ignorance, his reason such,
Whether he thinks too little, or too much:
Chaos of Thought and Passion, all confus'd;
Still by himself abus'd, or disabus'd;
Created half to rise, and half to fall;
Great lord of all things, yet a prey to all;
Sole judge of Truth, in endless Error hurl'd:
The glory, jest, and riddle of the world!

E. E. CUMMINGS

from spiralling ecstatically this

from spiralling ecstatically this

proud nowhere of earth's most prodigious night
blossoms a newborn babe:around him,eyes
—gifted with every keener appetite
than mere unmiracle can quite appease—
humbly in their imagined bodies kneel
(over time space doom dream while floats the whole

perhapsless mystery of paradise)

mind without soul may blast some universe
to might have been,and stop ten thousand stars
but not one heartbeat of this child;nor shall
even prevail a million questionings
against the silence of his mother's smile

—whose only secret all creation sings

Theodore Roethke

The Waking

I wake to sleep, and take my waking slow.
I feel my fate in what I cannot fear.
I learn by going where I have to go.

We think by feeling. What is there to know?
I hear my being dance from ear to ear.
I wake to sleep, and take my waking slow.

Of those so close beside me, which are you?
God bless the Ground! I shall walk softly there,
And learn by going where I have to go.

Light takes the Tree; but who can tell us how?
The lowly worm climbs up a winding stair;
I wake to sleep, and take my waking slow.

Great Nature has another thing to do
To you and me; so take the lively air,
And, lovely, learn by going where to go.

This shaking keeps me steady. I should know.
What falls away is always. And is near.
I wake to sleep, and take my waking slow.
I learn by going where I have to go.

The Choice

Think thou and act; to-morrow thou shalt die.
   Outstretched in the sun's warmth upon the shore,
   Thou say'st: 'Man's measured path is all gone o'er:
Up all his years, steeply, with strain and sigh,
Man clomb until he touched the truth; and I,
   Even I, am he whom it was destined for.'
   How should this be? Art thou then so much more
Than they who sowed, that thou shouldst reap thereby?

Nay, come up hither. From this wave-washed mound
   Unto the furthest flood-brim look with me;
Then reach on with thy thought till it be drown'd.
   Miles and miles distant though the grey line be,
And though thy soul sail leagues and leagues beyond, —
   Still, leagues beyond those leagues, there is more sea.

WALT WHITMAN

There Was a Child Went Forth

There was a child went forth every day,
And the first object he look'd upon, that object he became,
And that object became part of him for the day or a certain part of
the day,
Or for many years or stretching cycles of years.

The early lilacs became part of this child,
And grass and white and red morning-glories, and white and red
clover, and the song of the phoebe-bird,
And the Third-month lambs and the sow's pink-faint litter, and the
mare's foal and the cow's calf,
And the noisy brood of the barnyard or the mire of the pond-side,
And the fish suspending themselves so curiously below there, and the
beautiful curious liquid,
And the water-plants with their graceful flat heads, all became part
of him.

The field-sprouts of Fourth-month and Fifth-month became part of
him,
Winter-grain sprouts and those of the light-yellow corn, and the escu-
lent roots of the garden,
And the apple-trees cover'd with blossoms and the fruit afterward,
and wood-berries, and the commonest weeds by the road,
And the old drunkard staggering home from the outhouse of the tavern
whence he had lately risen,
And the schoolmistress that pass'd on her way to the school,
And the friendly boys that pass'd, and the quarrelsome boys,
And the tidy and fresh-cheek'd girls, and the barefoot negro boy and
girl,
And all the changes of city and country wherever he went.

His own parents, he that had father'd him and she that had conceiv'd
  him in her womb and birth'd him,
They gave this child more of themselves than that,
They gave him afterward every day, they became part of him.
The mother at home quietly placing the dishes on the supper-table,
The mother with mild words, clean her cap and gown, a wholesome
  odor falling off her person and clothes as she walks by,
The father, strong, self-sufficient, manly, mean, anger'd, unjust,
The blow, the quick loud word, the tight bargain, the crafty lure,
The family usages, the language, the company, the furniture, the
  yearning and swelling heart,
Affection that will not be gainsay'd, the sense of what is real, the
  thought if after all it should prove unreal,
The doubts of day-time and the doubts of night-time, the curious
  whether and how,
Whether that which appears so is so, or is it all flashes and specks?
Men and women crowding fast in the streets, if they are not flashes
  and specks what are they?
The streets themselves and the façades of houses, and goods in the
  windows,
Vehicles, teams, the heavy-plank'd wharves, the huge crossing at the
  ferries,
The village on the highland seen from afar at sunset, the river between,
Shadows, aureola and mist, the light falling on roofs and gables of
  white or brown two miles off,
The schooner near by sleepily dropping down the tide, the little boat
  slack-tow'd astern,
The hurrying tumbling waves, quick-broken crests, slapping,
The strata of color'd clouds, the long bar of maroon-tint away solitary
  by itself, the spread of purity it lies motionless in,
The horizon's edge, the flying sea-crow, the fragrance of salt marsh
  and shore mud,
These became part of that child who went forth every day, and who
  now goes, and will always go forth every day.

ALLEN GINSBERG

Wild Orphan

Blandly mother
takes him strolling
    by railroad and by river
— he's the son of the absconded
    hot rod angel —
and he imagines cars
    and rides them in his dreams,

so lonely growing up among
    the imaginary automobiles
and dead souls of Tarrytown

    to create
out of his own imagination
    the beauty of his wild
forebears — a mythology
    he cannot inherit.

Will he later hallucinate
    his gods? Waking
among mysteries with
    an insane gleam
of recollection?

    The recognition —
something so rare
    in his soul,
met only in dreams
    — nostalgias
of another life.

A question of the soul.
    And the injured
losing their injury
    in their innocence
— a cock, a cross,
    an excellence of love.

And the father grieves
    in flophouse
complexities of memory
    a thousand miles
away, unknowing
    of the unexpected
youthful stranger
    bumming toward his door.

Robert Frost

The Road Not Taken

Two roads diverged in a yellow wood,
And sorry I could not travel both
And be one traveler, long I stood
And looked down one as far as I could
To where it bent in the undergrowth;

Then took the other, as just as fair,
And having perhaps the better claim,
Because it was grassy and wanted wear;
Though as for that the passing there
Had worn them really about the same,

And both that morning equally lay
In leaves no step had trodden black.
Oh, I kept the first for another day!
Yet knowing how way leads on to way,
I doubted if I should ever come back.

I shall be telling this with a sigh
Somewhere ages and ages hence:
Two roads diverged in a wood, and I —
I took the one less traveled by,
And that has made all the difference.

SAMUEL TAYLOR COLERIDGE

Time, Real and Imaginary

An Allegory

On the wide level of a mountain's head,
(I knew not where, but 'twas some faery place)
Their pinions, ostrich-like, for sails out-spread,
Two lovely children run an endless race,
    A sister and a brother!
    This far outstripp'd the other;
    Yet ever runs she with reverted face,
    And looks and listens for the boy behind:
    For he, alas! is blind!
O'er rough and smooth with even step he passed,
And knows not whether he be first or last.

Dylan Thomas

The Force That Through the Green Fuse Drives the Flower

The force that through the green fuse drives the flower
Drives my green age; that blasts the roots of trees
Is my destroyer.
And I am dumb to tell the crooked rose
My youth is bent by the same wintry fever.

The force that drives the water through the rocks
Drives my red blood; that dries the mouthing streams
Turns mine to wax.
And I am dumb to mouth unto my veins
How at the mountain spring the same mouth sucks.

The hand that whirls the water in the pool
Stirs the quicksand; that ropes the blowing wind
Hauls my shroud sail.
And I am dumb to tell the hanging man
How of my clay is made the hangman's lime.

The lips of time leech to the fountain head;
Love drips and gathers, but the fallen blood
Shall calm her sores.
And I am dumb to tell a weather's wind
How time has ticked a heaven round the stars.

And I am dumb to tell the lover's tomb
How at my sheet goes the same crooked worm.

WALTER SAVAGE LANDOR

The Dragon-fly

Life (priest and poet say) is but a dream;
    I wish no happier one than to be laid
    Beneath a cool syringa's scented shade,
Or wavy willow, by the running stream,
    Brimful of moral, where the dragon-fly,
    Wanders as careless and content as I.
Thanks for this fancy, insect king,
Of purple crest and filmy wing,
Who with indifference givest up
The water-lily's golden cup,
To come again and overlook
What I am writing in my book.
Believe me, most who read the line
Will read with hornier eyes than thine;
And yet their souls shall live for ever,
And thine drop dead into the river!
God pardon them, O insect king,
Who fancy so unjust a thing!

Alfred, Lord Tennyson

The Eagle

Fragment

He clasps the crag with crooked hands;
Close to the sun in lonely lands,
Ring'd with the azure world, he stands.

The wrinkled sea beneath him crawls;
He watches from his mountain walls,
And like a thunderbolt he falls.

WILLIAM MORRIS

March

Slayer of the winter, art thou here again?
O welcome, thou that bring'st the summer nigh!
The bitter wind makes not thy victory vain,
Nor will we mock thee for thy faint blue sky.
Welcome, O March! whose kindly days and dry
Make April ready for the throstle's song,
Thou first redresser of the winter's wrong!

Yea, welcome March! and though I die ere June,
Yet for the hope of life I give thee praise,
Striving to swell the burden of the tune
That even now I hear thy brown birds raise,
Unmindful of the past or coming days;
Who sing: "O joy! a new year is begun:
What happiness to look upon the sun!"

Ah, what begetteth all this storm of bliss
But Death himself, who crying solemnly,
E'en from the heart of sweet Forgetfulness,
Bids us "Rejoice, lest pleasureless ye die.
Within a little time must ye go by.
Stretch forth your open hands, and while ye live
Take all the gifts that Death and Life may give."

Before the Mirror

I

White rose in red rose-garden
   Is not so white;
Snowdrops that plead for pardon
   And pine for fright
Because the hard East blows
Over their maiden rows
   Grow not as this face grows from pale to bright.

Behind the veil, forbidden
   Shut up from sight,
Lover, is there sorrow hidden,
   Is there delight?
Is joy thy dower of grief,
White rose of weary leaf,
   Late rose whose life is brief, whose loves are light?

Soft snows that hard winds harden
   Till each flake bite
Fill all the flowerless garden
   Whose flowers took flight
Long since when summer ceased,
And men rose up from feast.
   And warm west wind grew east, and warm day night.

II

"Come snow, come wind or thunder
   High up in air,
I watch my face, and wonder

At my bright hair;
Nought else exalts or grieves
The rose at heart, that heaves
    With love of her own leaves and lips that pair.

"She knows not loves that kissed her
    She knows not where,
Art thou the ghost, my sister,
    White sister there,
Am I the ghost, who knows?
My hand, a fallen rose,
    Lies snow-white on white snows, and takes no care.

"I cannot see what pleasures
    Or what pains were;
What pale new loves and treasures
    New years will bear;
What beam will fall, what shower,
What grief or joy for dower;
    But one thing knows the flower; the flower is fair."

III

Glad, but not flushed with gladness,
    Since joys go by;
Sad, but not bent with sadness,
    Since sorrows die;
Deep in the gleaming glass
She sees all past things pass,
    And all sweet life that was lie down and lie.

There glowing ghosts of flowers
    Draw down, draw nigh;
And wings of swift spent hours
    Take flight and fly;

She sees by formless gleams,
She hears across cold streams,
    Dead mouths of many dreams that sing and sigh.

Face fallen and white throat lifted,
    With sleepless eye
She sees old loves that drifted,
    She knew not why,
Old loves and faded fears
Float down a stream that hears
    The flowing of all men's tears beneath the sky.

WILLIAM COWPER

The Poplar Field

The poplars are felled, farewell to the shade
And the whispering sound of the cool colonnade,
The winds play no longer, and sing in the leaves,
Nor Ouse on his bosom their image receives.

Twelve years have elapsed since I first took a view
Of my favorite field and the bank where they grew,
And now in the grass behold they are laid,
And the tree is my seat that once lent me a shade.

The blackbird has fled to another retreat
Where the hazels afford him a screen from the heat,
And the scene where his melody charmed me before,
Resounds with his sweet-flowing ditty no more.

My fugitive years are all hasting away,
And I must ere long lie as lowly as they,
With a turf on my breast, and a stone at my head,
Ere another such grove shall arise in its stead.

'Tis a sight to engage me, if any thing can,
To muse on the perishing pleasures of man;
Though his life be a dream, his enjoyments, I see,
Have a being less durable even than he.

GERARD MANLEY HOPKINS

Pied Beauty

Glory be to God for dappled things —
   For skies of couple-colour as a brinded cow;
      For rose-moles all in stipple upon trout that swim;
Fresh-firecoal chestnut-falls; finches' wings;
   Landscape plotted and pieced — fold, fallow, and plough;
      And áll trádes, their gear and tackle and trim.

All things counter, original, spare, strange;
   Whatever is fickle, freckled (who knows how?)
      With swift, slow; sweet, sour; adazzle, dim;
He fathers-forth whose beauty is past change:
                    Praise him.

JONATHAN SWIFT

A Description of the Morning

Now hardly here and there a hackney coach
Appearing, showed the ruddy morn's approach.
Now Betty from her master's bed had flown,
And softly stole to discompose her own;
The slip-shod 'prentice from his master's door
Had pared the dirt and sprinkled round the floor.
Now Moll had whirled her mop with dext'rous airs,
Prepared to scrub the entry and the stairs.
The youth with broomy stumps began to trace
The kennel's edge, where wheels had worn the place.
The small-coal man was heard with cadence deep,
Till drowned in shriller notes of chimney-sweep:
Duns at his lordship's gate began to meet;
And brickdust Moll had screamed through half the street.
The turnkey now his flock returning sees,
Duly let out a-nights to steal for fees:
The watchful bailiffs take their silent stands,
And schoolboys lag with satchels in their hands.

Lawrence Ferlinghetti
Constantly Risking Absurdity

Constantly risking absurdity
              and death
    whenever he performs
           above the heads
                of his audience
  the poet like an acrobat
      climbs on rime
          to a high wire of his own making
and balancing on eyebeams
        above a sea of faces
    paces his way
        to the other side of day
   performing entrechats
        and sleight-of-foot tricks
  and other high theatrics
        and all without mistaking
    any thing
      for what it may not be

  For he's the super realist
        who must perforce perceive
    taut truth
        before the taking of each stance or step
in his supposed advance
        toward that still higher perch
where Beauty stands and waits
      with gravity
        to start her death-defying leap

And he
      a little charleychaplin man
                  who may or may not catch
     her fair eternal form
            spreadeagled in the empty air
      of existence

Samuel Johnson

To Miss ——

*On Her Playing upon the Harpsichord
in a Room Hung with Some Flower-Pieces
of Her Own Painting*

When Stella strikes the tuneful string
In scenes of imitated spring,
Where Beauty lavishes her powers
On beds of never-fading flowers,
And pleasure propagates around
Each charm of modulated sound,
Ah! think not, in the dangerous hour,
The nymph fictitious, as the flower;
But shun, rash youth, the gay alcove,
Nor tempt the snares of wily love.

When charms thus press on every sense,
What thought of flight, or of defense?
Deceitful Hope, and vain Desire,
Forever flutter o'er her lyre,
Delighting, as the youth draws nigh,
To point the glances of her eye,
And forming, with unerring art,
New chains to hold the captive heart.

But on these regions of delight,
Might Truth intrude with daring flight,
Could Stella, sprightly, fair and young,
One moment hear the moral song,
Instruction with her flowers might spring,
And Wisdom warble from her string.

Mark, when from thousand mingled dyes
Thou see'st one pleasing form arise,
How active light, and thoughtful shade,

In greater scenes each other aid;
Mark, when the different notes agree
In friendly contrariety,
How passion's well-accorded strife
Gives all the harmony of life;
Thy pictures shall thy conduct frame,
Consistent still, though not the same,
Thy music teach the nobler art
To tune the regulated heart.

WILLIAM BLAKE

London

I wander thro' each charter'd street,
Near where the charter'd Thames does flow,
And mark in every face I meet
Marks of weakness, marks of woe.

In every cry of every Man,
In every Infant's cry of fear,
In every voice, in every ban,
The mind-forg'd manacles I hear.

How the Chimney-sweeper's cry
Every black'ning Church appalls;
And the hapless Soldier's sigh
Runs in blood down Palace walls.

But most thro' midnight streets I hear
How the youthful Harlot's curse
Blasts the new born Infant's tear,
And blights with plagues the Marriage hearse.

Henry Howard, Earl of Surrey

The Means to Attain Happy Life

Martial, the things that do attain
 The happy life be these, I find:
The richesse left, not got with pain;
 The fruitful ground, the quiet mind;

The equal friend; no grudge, no strife;
 No charge of rule, nor governance;
Without disease, the healthful life;
 The household of continuance;

The mean diet, no delicate fare;
 True wisdom join'd with simpleness;
The night dischargèd of all care,
 Where wine the wit may not oppress.

The faithful wife, without debate;
 Such sleeps as may beguile the night:
Contented with thine own estate
 Nor wish for death, nor fear his might.

WILLIAM WORDSWORTH

Miscellaneous Sonnet XXXVI

Composed upon Westminster Bridge, September 3, 1802

Earth has not anything to show more fair:
Dull would he be of soul who could pass by
A sight so touching in its majesty:
This City now doth, like a garment, wear
The beauty of the morning; silent, bare,
Ships, towers, domes, theatres, and temples lie
Open unto the fields, and to the sky;
All bright and glittering in the smokeless air.
Never did sun more beautifully steep
In his first splendour, valley, rock, or hill;
Ne'er saw I, never felt, a calm so deep!
The river glideth at his own sweet will:
Dear God! the very houses seem asleep;
And all that mighty heart is lying still!

W. H. Auden

The City

In villages from which their childhoods came
Seeking Necessity, they had been taught
Necessity by nature is the same,
No matter how or by whom it be sought.

The city, though, assumed no such belief,
But welcomed each as if he came alone,
The nature of Necessity like grief
Exactly corresponding to his own.

And offered them so many, every one
Found some temptation fit to govern him;
And settled down to master the whole craft

Of being nobody; sat in the sun
During the lunch-hour round the fountain rim;
And watched the country kids arrive, and laughed.

ARNA BONTEMPS

Southern Mansion

Poplars are standing there still as death
And ghosts of dead men
Meet their ladies walking
Two by two beneath the shade
And standing on the marble steps.

There is a sound of music echoing
Through the open door
And in the field there is
Another sound tinkling in the cotton:
Chains of bondmen dragging on the ground.

The years go back with an iron clank,
A hand is on the gate,
A dry leaf trembles on the wall.
Ghosts are walking.
They have broken roses down
And poplars stand there still as death.

Rudyard Kipling

The Way Through the Woods

They shut the road through the woods
Seventy years ago.
Weather and rain have undone it again,
And now you would never know
There was once a road through the woods
Before they planted the trees.
It is underneath the coppice and heath,
And the thin anemones.
Only the keeper sees
That, where the ring-dove broods,
And the badgers roll at ease,
There was once a road through the woods.

Yet, if you enter the woods
Of a summer evening late,
When the night-air cools on the trout-ringed pools
Where the otter whistles his mate,
(They fear not men in the woods,
Because they see so few.)
You will hear the beat of a horse's feet,
And the swish of a skirt in the dew,
Steadily cantering through
The misty solitudes,
As though they perfectly knew
The old lost road through the woods. . . .
But there is no road through the woods.

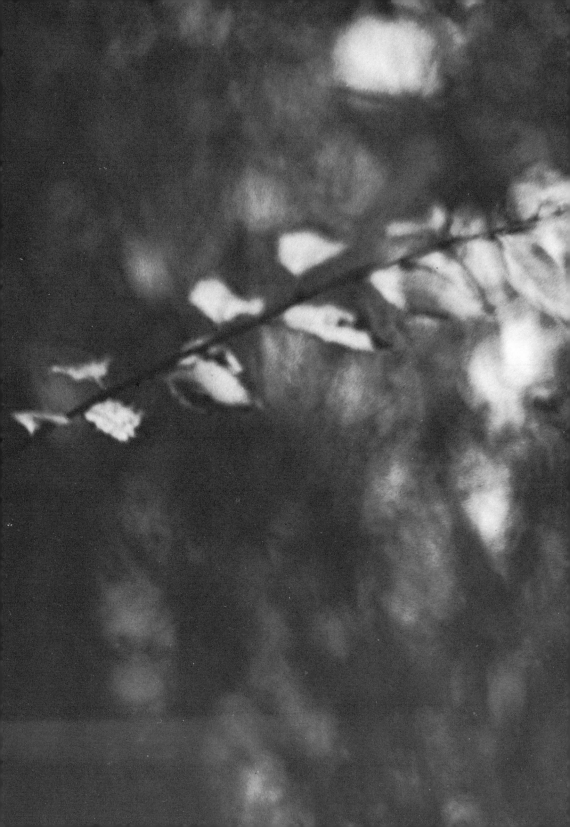

Jay Wright

This Morning

This morning I threw the windows
of my room open, the light burst
in like crystal gauze and I hung
it on my wall to frame.
And here I am watching it take possession
of my room, watching the obscure love
match of light and shadow — of cold and warmth.
It is a matter of acceptance, I guess.
It is a matter of finding some room
with shadows to embrace, open. Now
the light has settled in, I don't think
I shall ever close my windows again.

GARY SNYDER

North Beach Alba

waking half-drunk in a strange pad
making it out to the cool gray
    san francisco dawn —
white gulls over white houses,
    fog down the bay,
tamalpais a fresh green hill in the new sun,
driving across the bridge in a beat old car
    to work.

The Trees in the Garden Rained Flowers

The trees in the garden rained flowers.
Children ran there joyously.
They gathered the flowers
Each to himself.
Now there were some
Who gathered great heaps —
Having opportunity and skill —
Until, behold, only chance blossoms
Remained for the feeble.
Then a little spindling tutor
Ran importantly to the father, crying:
"Pray, come hither!
"See this unjust thing in your garden!"
But when the father had surveyed,
He admonished the tutor:
"Not so, small sage!
"This thing is just.
"For, look you,
"Are not they who possess the flowers
"Stronger, bolder, shrewder
"Than they who have none?
"Why should the strong —
"The beautiful strong —
"Why should they not have the flowers?"

Upon reflection, the tutor bowed to the ground.
"My lord," he said,
"The stars are displaced
"By this towering wisdom."

EMILY DICKINSON

I'm Nobody! Who Are You?

I'm Nobody! Who are you?
Are you – Nobody – Too?
Then there's a pair of us?
Don't tell! they'd advertise – you know!

How dreary – to be – Somebody!
How public – like a Frog –
To tell one's name – the livelong June –
To an admiring Bog!

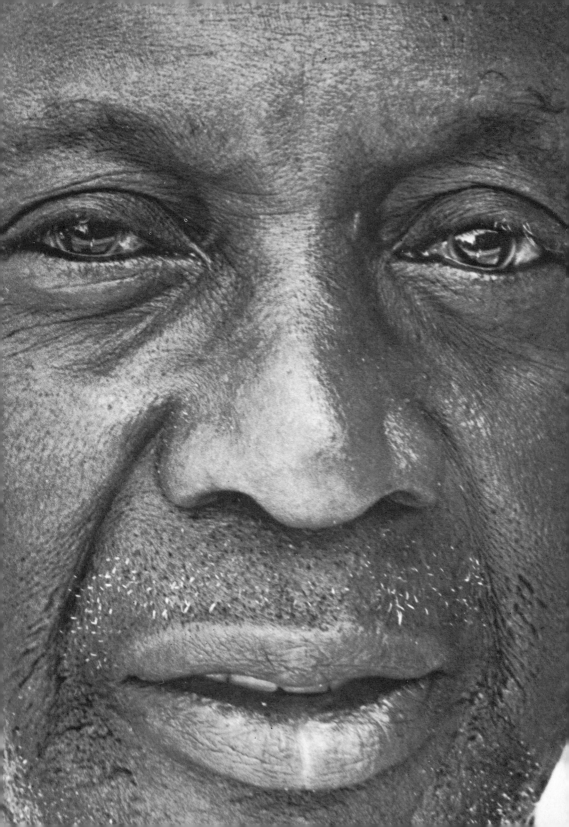

Ray Durem

Award

A Gold Watch to the FBI Man
who has followed me
for 25 Years.

Well, old spy
looks like I
led you down some pretty blind alleys,
took you on several trips to Mexico,
fishing in the high Sierras,
jazz at the Philharmonic.
You've watched me all your life,
I've clothed your wife,
put your two sons through college.
what good has it done?
the sun keeps rising every morning.
ever see me buy an Assistant President?
or close a school?
or lend money to Trujillo?
ever catch me rigging airplane prices?
I bought some after-hours whiskey in L.A.
but the Chief got his pay.
I ain't killed no Koreans
or fourteen-year-old boys in Mississippi.
neither did I bomb Guatemala,
or lend guns to shoot Algerians.
I admit I took a Negro child
to a white rest room in Texas,
but she was my daughter, only three,
who had to pee.

Hart Crane

Chaplinesque

We make our meek adjustments,
Contented with such random consolations
As the wind deposits
In slithered and too ample pockets.

For we can still love the world, who find
A famished kitten on the step, and know
Recesses for it from the fury of the street,
Or warm torn elbow coverts.

We will sidestep, and to the final smirk
Dally the doom of that inevitable thumb
That slowly chafes its puckered index toward us,
Facing the dull squint with what innocence
And what surprise!

And yet these fine collapses are not lies
More than the pirouettes of any pliant cane;
Our obsequies are, in a way, no enterprise.
We can evade you, and all else but the heart:
What blame to us if the heart live on.

The game enforces smirks; but we have seen
The moon in lonely alleys make
A grail of laughter of an empty ash can,
And through all sound of gaiety and quest
Have heard a kitten in the wilderness.

John Clare

Written in Northampton County Asylum

I am! yet what I am who cares, or knows?
   My friends forsake me like a memory lost.
I am the self-consumer of my woes;
   They rise and vanish, an oblivious host,
Shadows of life, whose very soul is lost.
And yet I am — I live — though I am toss'd

Into the nothingness of scorn and noise,
   Into the living sea of waking dream,
Where there is neither sense of life, nor joys,
   But the huge shipwreck of my own esteem
And all that's dear. Even those I loved the best
Are strange — nay, they are stranger than the rest.

I long for scenes where man has never trod —
   For scenes where woman never smiled or wept —
There to abide with my Creator, God,
   And sleep as I in childhood sweetly slept,
Full of high thoughts, unborn. So let me lie, —
The grass below; above, the vaulted sky.

WILLIAM ERNEST HENLEY

Discharged

Carry me out
Into the wind and the sunshine,
Into the beautiful world.

O, the wonder, the spell of the streets!
The stature and strength of the horses,
The rustle and echo of footfalls,
The flat roar and rattle of wheels!
A swift tram floats huge on us . . .
It's a dream?
The smell of the mud in my nostrils
Blows brave — like a breath of the sea!

As of old,
Ambulant, undulant drapery,
Vaguely and strangely provocative,
Flutters and beckons. O, yonder —
Is it? — the gleam of a stocking!
Sudden, a spire
Wedged in the mist! O, the houses,
The long lines of lofty, grey houses,
Cross-hatched with shadow and light!
These are the streets. . . .
Each is an avenue leading
Whither I will!

Free . . . !
Dizzy, hysterical, faint,
I sit, and the carriage rolls on with me
Into the wonderful world.

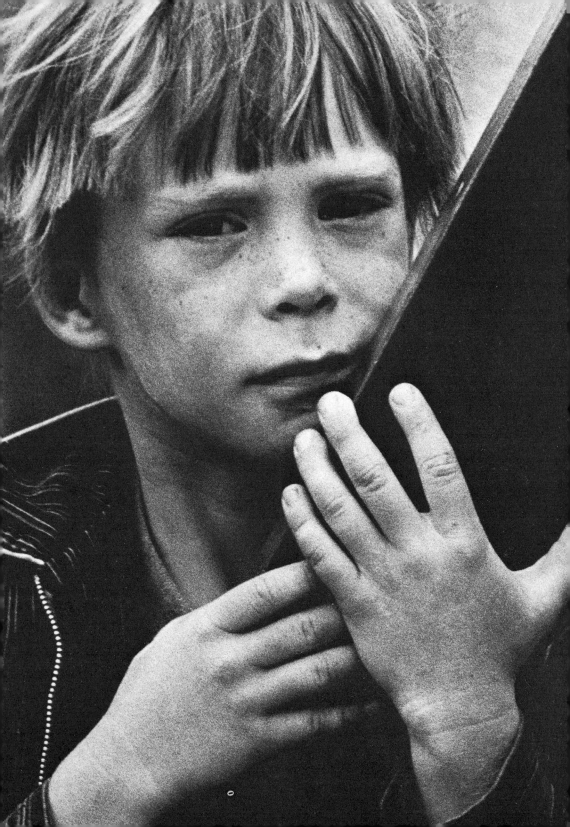

Sylvia Plath

Daddy

You do not do, you do not do
Any more, black shoe
In which I have lived like a foot
For thirty years, poor and white,
Barely daring to breathe or Achoo.

Daddy, I have had to kill you.
You died before I had time —
Marble-heavy, a bag full of God,
Ghastly statue with one grey toe
Big as a Frisco seal

And a head in the freakish Atlantic
Where it pours bean green over blue
In the waters off beautiful Nauset.
I used to pray to recover you.
Ach, du.

In the German tongue, in the Polish town
Scraped flat by the roller
Of wars, wars, wars.
But the name of the town is common.
My Polack friend

Says there are a dozen or two.
So I never could tell where you
Put your foot, your root,
I never could talk to you.
The tongue stuck in my jaw.

It stuck in a barb wire snare.
Ich, ich, ich, ich,
I could hardly speak.
I thought every German was you.
And the language obscene

An engine, an engine
Chuffing me off like a Jew.
A Jew to Dachau, Auschwitz, Belsen.
I began to talk like a Jew.
I think I may well be a Jew.

The snows of the Tyrol, the clear beer of Vienna
Are not very pure or true.
With my gypsy ancestress and my weird luck
And my Taroc pack and my Taroc pack
I may be a bit of a Jew.

I have always been scared of *you*,
With your Luftwaffe, your gobbledygoo.
And your neat moustache
And your Aryan eye, bright blue.
Panzer-man, panzer-man, O You —

Not God but a swastika
So black no sky could squeak through.
Every woman adores a Fascist,
The boot in the face, the brute
Brute heart of a brute like you.

You stand at the blackboard, daddy,
In the picture I have of you,
A cleft in your chin instead of your foot
But no less a devil for that, no not
Any less the black man who

Bit my pretty red heart in two.
I was ten when they buried you.
At twenty I tried to die
And get back, back, back to you.
I thought even the bones would do.

But they pulled me out of the sack,
And they stuck me together with glue.
And then I knew what to do.
I made a model of you,
A man in black with a Meinkampf look

And a love of the rack and the screw.
And I said I do, I do.
So daddy, I'm finally through.
The black telephone's off at the root,
The voices just can't worm through.

If I've killed one man, I've killed two —
The vampire who said he was you
And drank my blood for a year,
Seven years, if you want to know.
Daddy, you can lie back now.

There's a stake in your fat black heart
And the villagers never liked you.
They are dancing and stamping on you.
They always *knew* it was you.
Daddy, daddy, you bastard, I'm through.

WALLACE STEVENS

The Motive for Metaphor

You like it under the trees in autumn,
Because everything is half dead.
The wind moves like a cripple among the leaves
And repeats words without meaning.

In the same way, you were happy in spring,
With the half colors of quarter-things,
The slightly brighter sky, the melting clouds,
The single bird, the obscure moon —

The obscure moon lighting an obscure world
Of things that would never be quite expressed,
Where you yourself were never quite yourself
And did not want nor have to be,

Desiring the exhilarations of changes:
The motive for metaphor, shrinking from
The weight of primary noon,
The A B C of being,

The ruddy temper, the hammer
Of red and blue, the hard sound —
Steel against intimation — the sharp flash,
The vital, arrogant, fatal, dominant X.

Sidney Lanier

Opposition

Of fret, of dark, of thorn, of chill,
    Complain no more; for these, O heart,
Direct the random of the will
    As rhymes direct the rage of art.

The lute's fixt fret, that runs athwart
    The strain and purpose of the string,
For governance and nice consort
    Doth bar his wilful wavering.

The dark hath many dear avails;
    The dark distils divinest dews;
The dark is rich with nightingales,
    With dreams, and with the heavenly Muse.

Bleeding with thorns of petty strife,
    I'll ease (as lovers do) my smart
With sonnets to my lady Life,
    Writ red in issues from the heart.

What grace may lie within the chill
    Of favor frozen fast in scorn!
When Good's a-freeze, we call it Ill!
    This rosy Time is glacier-born.

Of fret, of dark, of thorn, of chill,
    Complain thou not, O heart; for these
Bank-in the current of the will
    To uses, arts, and charities.

RALPH WALDO EMERSON

Brahma

If the red slayer think he slays,
   Or if the slain think he is slain,
They know not well the subtle ways
   I keep, and pass, and turn again.

Far or forgot to me is near;
   Shadow and sunlight are the same;
The vanished gods to me appear;
   And one to me are shame and fame.

They reckon ill who leave me out;
   When me they fly, I am the wings;
I am the doubter and the doubt,
   And I the hymn the Brahmin sings.

The strong gods pine for my abode,
   And pine in vain the sacred Seven;
But thou, meek lover of the good!
   Find me, and turn thy back on heaven.

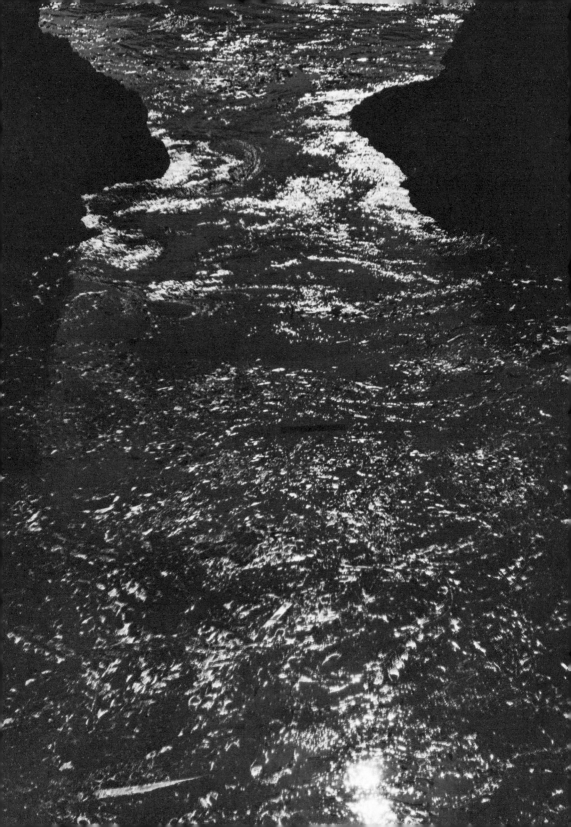

Dover Beach

The sea is calm to-night.
The tide is full, the moon lies fair
Upon the straits; — on the French coast the light
Gleams and is gone; the cliffs of England stand,
Glimmering and vast, out in the tranquil bay.
Come to the window, sweet is the night-air!
Only, from the long line of spray
Where the sea meets the moon-blanch'd land,
Listen! you hear the grating roar
Of pebbles which the waves draw back, and fling,
At their return, up the high strand,
Begin, and cease, and then again begin,
With tremulous cadence slow, and bring
The eternal note of sadness in.

Sophocles long ago
Heard it on the Aegaean, and it brought
Into his mind the turbid ebb and flow
Of human misery; we
Find also in the sound a thought,
Hearing it by this distant northern sea.

The Sea of Faith
Was once, too, at the full, and round earth's shore
Lay like the folds of a bright girdle furl'd.
But now I only hear
Its melancholy, long, withdrawing roar,
Retreating, to the breath
Of the night-wind, down the vast edges drear
And naked shingles of the world.

Ah, love, let us be true
To one another! for the world, which seems
To lie before us like a land of dreams,
So various, so beautiful, so new,
Hath really neither joy, nor love, nor light,
Nor certitude, nor peace, nor help for pain;
And we are here as on a darkling plain
Swept with confused alarms of struggle and flight,
Where ignorant armies clash by night.

Robert Lowell

Skunk Hour

(For Elizabeth Bishop)

Nautilus Island's hermit
heiress still lives through winter in her Spartan cottage;
her sheep still graze above the sea.
Her son's a bishop. Her farmer
is first selectman in our village;
she's in her dotage.

Thirsting for
the hierarchic privacy
of Queen Victoria's century,
she buys up all
the eyesores facing her shore,
and lets them fall.

The season's ill —
we've lost our summer millionaire,
who seemed to leap from an L. L. Bean
catalogue. His nine-knot yawl
was auctioned off to lobstermen.
A red fox stain covers Blue Hill.

And now our fairy
decorator brightens his shop for fall;
his fishnet's filled with orange cork,
orange, his cobbler's bench and awl;
there is no money in his work,
he'd rather marry.

One dark night,
my Tudor Ford climbed the hill's skull;
I watched for love-cars. Lights turned down,
they lay together, hull to hull,
where the graveyard shelves on the town. . . .
My mind's not right.

A car radio bleats,
"Love, O careless Love. . . ." I hear
my ill-spirit sob in each blood cell,
as if my hand were at its throat. . . .
I myself am hell;
nobody's here —

only skunks, that search
in the moonlight for a bite to eat.
They march on their soles up Main Street:
white stripes, moonstruck eyes' red fire
under the chalk-dry and spar spire
of the Trinitarian Church.

I stand on top
of our back steps and breathe the rich air —
a mother skunk with her column of kittens swills the garbage pail.
She jabs her wedge-head in a cup
of sour cream, drops her ostrich tail,
and will not scare.

OLIVER ST. JOHN GOGARTY

The Image-Maker

Hard is the stone, but harder still
The delicate preforming will
That guided by a dream alone,
Subdues and moulds the hardest stone,
Making the stubborn jade release
The emblem of eternal peace.

If but the will be firmly bent,
No stuff resists the mind's intent;
The adamant abets his skill
And sternly aids the artist's will,
To clothe in perdurable pride
Beauty his transient eyes descried.

John Milton

XIX   On His Blindness

When I consider how my light is spent,
    Ere half my days, in this dark world and wide,
    And that one talent which is death to hide,
    Lodged with me useless, though my soul more bent
To serve therewith my maker, and present
    My true account, lest he returning chide,
    'Doth God exact day-labor, light denied,'
    I fondly ask; But patience to prevent
That murmur, soon replies, 'God doth not need
    Either man's work or his own gifts, who best
    Bear his mild yoke, they serve him best, his state
Is kingly. Thousands at his bidding speed
    And post o'er land and ocean without rest:
    They also serve who only stand and wait.'

JAMES HENRY LEIGH HUNT

Abou Ben Adhem

Abou Ben Adhem (may his tribe increase)
Awoke one night from a deep dream of peace,
And saw — within the moonlight in his room,
Making it rich and like a lily in bloom —
An angel, writing in a book of gold.
Exceeding peace had made Ben Adhem bold,
And to the presence in the room he said,
'What writest thou?' — The vision raised its head,
And, with a look made of all sweet accord,
Answered, 'The names of those who love the Lord.'
'And is mine one?' said Abou. 'Nay, not so,'
Replied the angel. Abou spoke more low,
But cheerly still, and said, 'I pray thee, then,
Write me as one that loves his fellow men.'

The angel wrote and vanished. The next night
It came again with a great wakening light,
And showed the names whom love of God had blessed,
And lo! Ben Adhem's name led all the rest.

Thomas Moore

The Light of Other Days

Oft, in the stilly night,
   Ere slumber's chain has bound me,
Fond Memory brings the light
   Of other days around me:
     The smiles, the tears
     Of boyhood's years,
   The words of love then spoken;
     The eyes that shone,
     Now dimm'd and gone,
   The cheerful hearts now broken!
Thus, in the stilly night,
   Ere slumber's chain has bound me,
Sad Memory brings the light
   Of other days around me.

When I remember all
   The friends, so link'd together,
I've seen around me fall
   Like leaves in wintry weather,
     I feel like one
     Who treads alone
   Some banquet-hall deserted,
     Whose lights are fled,
     Whose garlands dead,
   And all but he departed!
Thus, in the stilly night,
   Ere slumber's chain has bound me.
Sad Memory brings the light
   Of other days around me.

Ernest Dowson

Vitae Summa Brevis Spem Nos Vetat Incohare Longam

They are not long, the weeping and the laughter,
  Love and desire and hate:
I think they have no portion in us after
  We pass the gate.

They are not long, the days of wine and roses:
  Out of a misty dream
Our path emerges for a while, then closes
  Within a dream.

Edgar Allan Poe

A Dream Within a Dream

Take this kiss upon the brow!
And, in parting from you now,
Thus much let me avow —
You are not wrong, who deem
That my days have been a dream;
Yet if Hope has flown away
In a night, or in a day,
In a vision, or in none,
Is it therefore the less *gone*?
All that we see or seem
Is but a dream within a dream.

I stand amid the roar
Of a surf-tormented shore,
And I hold within my hand
Grains of the golden sand —
How few! yet how they creep
Through my fingers to the deep,
While I weep — while I weep!
O God! can I not grasp
Them with a tighter clasp?
O God! can I not save
One from the pitiless wave?
Is *all* that we see or seem
But a dream within a dream?

Thomas Hardy

Hap

If but some vengeful god would call to me
From up the sky, and laugh: "Thou suffering thing,
Know that thy sorrow is my ecstasy,
That thy love's loss is my hate's profiting!"

Then would I bear it, clench myself, and die,
Steeled by the sense of ire unmerited;
Half-eased in that a Powerfuller than I
Had willed and meted me the tears I shed.

But not so. How arrives it joy lies slain,
And why unblooms the best hope ever sown?
— Crass Casualty obstructs the sun and rain,
And dicing Time for gladness casts a moan. . . .
These purblind Doomsters had as readily strown
Blisses about my pilgrimage as pain.

KENNETH REXROTH

On What Planet

Uniformly over the whole countryside
The warm air flows imperceptibly seaward;
The autumn haze drifts in deep bands
Over the pale water;
White egrets stand in the blue marshes;
Tamalpais, Diablo, St. Helena
Float in the air.
Climbing on the cliffs of Hunter's Hill
We look out over fifty miles of sinuous
Interpenetration of mountains and sea.

Leading up a twisted chimney,
Just as my eyes rise to the level
Of a small cave, two white owls
Fly out, silent, close to my face.
They hover, confused in the sunlight,
And disappear into the recesses of the cliff.

All day I have been watching a new climber,
A young girl with ash blond hair
And gentle confident eyes.
She climbs slowly, precisely,
With unwasted grace.
While I am coiling the ropes,
Watching the spectacular sunset,
She turns to me and says, quietly,
"It must be very beautiful, the sunset,
On Saturn, with the rings and all the moons."

William Everson (Brother Antoninus)

Fish-Eaters

This blood has beat in a thousand veins,
And mingled redly in too many limbs
To remember the source, the single spring,
The fountain lost in the mist of the years.
Nordic and Celtic is all I know:
Pale-haired giants roaring their mirth on the Norway coast;
Somber Celts in the Irish fog,
Under the edge of the weedy dunes,
Huddling the meager blaze, and no singing.

I think of the men behind the centuries,
Groping down to the sea,
Fish-eaters, pickers of flesh from the salty shells,
Snuffling the wind of the water's edge, the black waves beating.
I think of the withered women left in the stinking huts of the hills,
No glimmer nor a hope,
And knowing no strength but the lips held mutely over the teeth.

O you folk of the farther dark,
This bone and this blood are nothing of mine,
But wrung from your flesh and fiercely born in the dimmest days,
When to live was to lust, to reach for the axe and rise to the fury,
Wade to the roaring thick of it,
Shoulders hunched and the long arms hacking.

Yet trying my heart I find no hunger for the sword,
This blood drowsy and slow, wanting no war,
Glad for the peace of the hawkless hills,
Glad for the sleep in the sun.

Siegfried Sassoon

In Me, Past, Present, Future Meet

In me, past, present, future meet
To hold long chiding conference.
My lusts usurp the present tense
And strangle Reason in his seat.
My loves leap through the future's fence
To dance with dream-enfranchised feet.

In me the cave-man clasps the seer,
And garlanded Apollo goes
Chanting to Abraham's deaf ear.
In me the tiger sniffs the rose.
    Look in my heart, kind friends, and tremble,
    Since there your elements assemble.

GEORGE HERBERT

Love

Love bade me welcome: yet my soul drew back,
      Guiltie of dust and sinne.
But quick-ey'd Love, observing me grow slack
      From my first entrance in,
Drew nearer to me, sweetly questioning,
      If I lack'd any thing.

A guest, I answer'd, worthy to be here:
      Love said, You shall be he.
I the unkinde, ungratefull? Ah my deare,
      I cannot look on thee.
Love took my hand, and smiling did reply,
      Who made the eyes but I?

Truth Lord, but I have marr'd them: let my shame
      Go where it doth deserve.
And know you not, sayes Love, who bore the blame?
      My deare, then I will serve.
You must sit down, sayes Love, and taste my meat:
      So I did sit and eat.

BEN JONSON

Caroline's Song

Though I am young, and cannot tell,
    Either what Death, or Love is well,
Yet I have heard, they both beare darts,
    And both doe ayme at humane hearts:
And then againe, I have beene told,
    Love wounds with heat, as Death with cold;
So that I feare, they doe but bring
    Extreames to touch, and meane one thing.

As in a ruine, we it call
    One thing to be blowne up, or fall;
Or to our end, like way may have,
    By a flash of lightning, or a wave:
So Loves inflamed shaft, or brand,
    May kill as soone as Deaths cold hand;
Except Loves fires the vertue have
    To fright the frost out of the grave.

Thomas Campion

Cherry-Ripe

There is a garden in her face,
　　Where roses and white lilies grow;
A heavenly paradise is that place,
　　Wherein all pleasant fruits do flow.
There cherries grow which none may buy,
Till 'Cherry-ripe' themselves do cry.

Those cherries fairly do enclose
　　Of orient pearl a double row,
Which when her lovely laughter shows,
　　They look like rosebuds filled with snow.
Yet them nor peer nor prince can buy,
Till 'Cherry-ripe' themselves do cry.

Her eyes like angels watch them still;
　　Her brows like bended bows do stand,
Threatening with piercing frowns to kill
　　All that attempt with eye or hand
Those sacred cherries to come nigh,
Till 'Cherry-ripe' themselves do cry.

EDMUND SPENSER

Sonnet LXVII

Lyke as a huntsman after weary chace,
  Seeing the game from him escapt away,
  sits downe to rest him in some shady place,
  with panting hounds beguiled of their pray:
So after long pursuit and vaine assay,
  when I all weary had the chace forsooke,
  the gentle deare returned the selfe-same way,
  thinking to quench her thirst at the next brooke.
There she beholding me with mylder looke,
  sought not to fly, but fearelesse still did bide:
  till I in hand her yet halfe trembling tooke,
  and with her owne goodwill hir fyrmely tyde.
Strange thing me seemd to see a beast so wyld,
  so goodly wonne with her owne will beguyld.

Song

Why so pale and wan fond lover?
    Prethee why so pale?
Will, when looking well can't move her
    Looking ill prevail?
    Prethee why so pale?

Why so dull and mute young sinner?
    Prethee why so mute?
Will, when speaking well can't win her?
    Saying nothing do 't?
    Prethee why so mute?

Quit, quit for shame, this will not move,
    This cannot take her;
If of her self she will not love,
    Nothing can make her:
    The divel take her.

ROBERT BURNS

O Were My Love Yon Lilac Fair

O were my Love yon lilac fair,
   Wi' purple blossoms to the spring,
And I a bird to shelter there,
   When wearied on my little wing;
How I wad mourn when it was torn
   By autumn wild and winter rude!
But I wad sing on wanton wing
   When youthfu' May its bloom renew'd.

O gin my Love were yon red rose
   That grows upon the castle wa',
And I mysel a drap o' dew,
   Into her bonnie breast to fa';
O there, beyond expression blest,
   I'd feast on beauty a' the night;
Seal'd on her silk-saft faulds to rest,
   Till fley'd awa' by Phoebus' light.

LEONARD COHEN

Suzanne

Suzanne takes you down to her place near the river
You can hear the boats go by
You can spend the night beside her
And you know that she's half crazy
But that's why you want to be there
And she feeds you tea and oranges
That come all the way from China
And just when you mean to tell her
That you have no love to give her
Then she gets you on her wavelength
And she lets the river answer
That you've always been her lover
And you want to travel with her
And you want to travel blind
And you know that she will trust you
For you've touched her perfect body with your mind.

And Jesus was a sailor
When he walked upon the water
And he spent a long time watching
From his lonely wooden tower
And when he knew for certain
Only drowning men could see him
He said "All men will be sailors then
Until the sea shall free them"
But he himself was broken
Long before the sky would open
Forsaken, almost human
He sank beneath your wisdom like a stone
And you want to travel with him

And you want to travel blind
And you think maybe you'll trust him
For he's touched your perfect body with his mind.

Now Suzanne takes your hand
And she leads you to the river
She is wearing rags and feathers
From Salvation Army counters
And the sun pours down like honey
On our lady of the harbour
And she shows you where to look
Among the garbage and the flowers
There are heroes in the seaweed
There are children in the morning
They are leaning out for love
And they will lean that way forever
While Suzanne holds the mirror
And you want to travel with her
And you want to travel blind
And you know you can trust her
For she's touched your perfect body with her mind.

PERCY BYSSHE SHELLEY

Lines

I

When the lamp is shattered,
The light in the dust lies dead;
When the cloud is scattered,
The rainbow's glory is shed;
When the lute is broken,
Sweet tones are remembered not;
When the lips have spoken,
Loved accents are soon forgot.

II

As music and splendor
Survive not the lamp and the lute,
The heart's echoes render
No song when the spirit is mute: —
No song but sad dirges,
Like the wind through a ruined cell,
Or the mournful surges
That ring the dead seaman's knell.

III

When hearts have once mingled,
Love first leaves the well-built nest;
The weak one is singled
To endure what it once possessed.
O Love! who bewailest
The frailty of all things here,
Why choose you the frailest
For your cradle, your home, and your bier?

IV

Its passions will rock thee,
As the storms rock the ravens on high;
　Bright reason will mock thee,
Like the sun from a wintry sky.
　From thy nest every rafter
Will rot, and thine eagle home
　Leave thee naked to laughter,
When leaves fall and cold winds come.

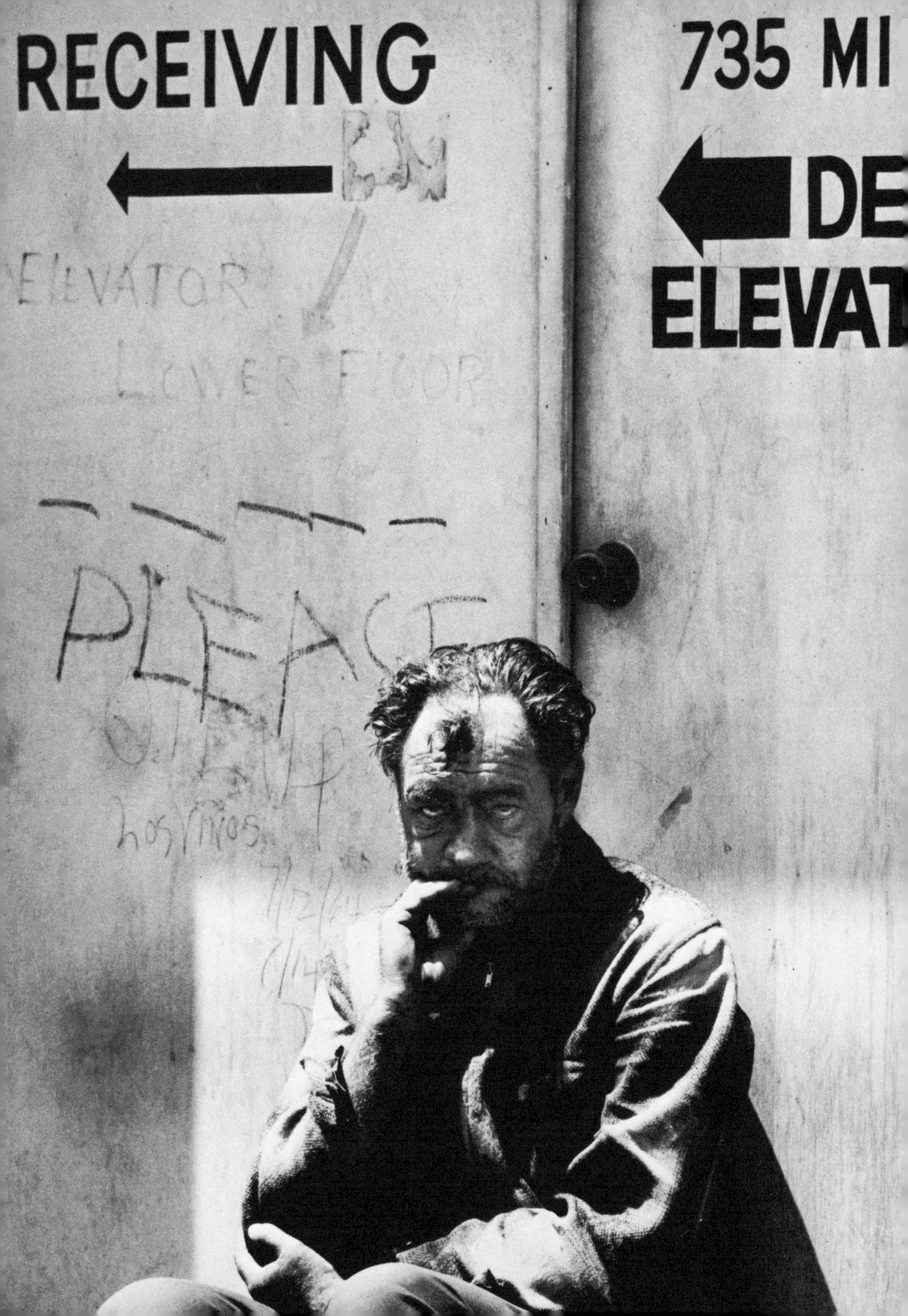
RECEIVING
735 MI
DE
ELEVAT

RICHARD LOVELACE

To Amarantha, That She Would Dishevel Her Hair

Amarantha sweet and fair,
Ah, braid no more that shining hair!
As my curious hand or eye
Hovering round thee, let it fly!

Let it fly as unconfined
As its calm ravisher the wind,
Who hath left his darling, th' East,
To wanton o'er that spicy nest.

Every tress must be confest,
But neatly tangled at the best;
Like a clew of golden thread
Most excellently ravellèd.

Do not then wind up that light
In ribbands, and o'ercloud in night,
Like the Sun in 's early ray;
But shake your head, and scatter day!

LORD BYRON

She Walks in Beauty

She walks in beauty, like the night
   Of cloudless climes and starry skies;
And all that 's best of dark and bright
   Meet in her aspect and her eyes:
Thus mellow'd to that tender light
   Which heaven to gaudy day denies.

One shade the more, one ray the less,
   Had half impair'd the nameless grace
Which waves in every raven tress,
   Or softly lightens o'er her face;
Where thoughts serenely sweet express
   How pure, how dear their dwelling-place.

And on that cheek, and o'er that brow,
   So soft, so calm, yet eloquent,
The smiles that win, the tints that glow,
   But tell of days in goodness spent,
A mind at peace with all below,
   A heart whose love is innocent!

John Dryden

Song to a Fair Young Lady

Going Out of the Town in the Spring

I

Ask not the cause, why sullen Spring
   So long delays her flow'rs to bear;
Why warbling birds forget to sing,
   And winter storms invert the year.
Chloris is gone, and fate provides
To make it spring where she resides.

II

Chloris is gone, the cruel fair:
   She cast not back a pitying eye;
But left her lover in despair,
   To sigh, to languish, and to die.
Ah, how can those fair eyes endure
To give the wounds they will not cure!

III

Great God of Love, why hast thou made
   A face that can all hearts command,
That all religions can invade,
   And change the laws of ev'ry land?
Where thou hadst plac'd such pow'r before,
Thou shouldst have made her mercy more.

IV

When Chloris to the temple comes,
   Adoring crowds before her fall:
She can restore the dead from tombs,
   And ev'ry life but mine recall.
I only am by Love design'd
To be the victim for mankind.

Sir Philip Sidney

Sonnet XLI

Having this day my horse, my hand, my launce
  Guided so well, that I obtain'd the prize,
  Both by the judgement of the English eyes,
And of some sent from that sweet enemie *Fraunce*;
Horsemen my skill in horsmanship advaunce;
  Towne-folkes my strength; a daintier judge applies
  His praise to sleight, which from good use doth rise;
Some luckie wits impute it but to chaunce;
  Others, because of both sides I do take
My bloud from them, who did excell in this,
Thinke Nature me a man of armes did make.
How farre they shoote awrie! the true cause is,
  Stella lookt on, and from her heavenly face
  Sent forth the beames, which made so faire my race.

WILLIAM DRUMMOND OF HAWTHORNDEN

Madrigal

The ivory, coral, gold,
Of breast, of lips, of hair,
So lively Sleep doth show to inward sight,
That wake I think I hold
No shadow, but my fair:
Myself so to deceive,
With long-shut eyes I shun the irksome light.
Such pleasure thus I have,
Delighting in false gleams,
If Death Sleep's brother be,
    And souls relieved of sense have so sweet dreams,
    That I would wish me thus to dream and die.

Ezra Pound

A Virginal

No, no! Go from me. I have left her lately.
I will not spoil my sheath with lesser brightness,
For my surrounding air hath a new lightness;
Slight are her arms, yet they have bound me straitly
And left me cloaked as with a gauze of aether;
As with sweet leaves; as with subtle clearness.
Oh, I have picked up magic in her nearness
To sheathe me half in half the things that sheathe her.
No, no! Go from me. I have still the flavour,
Soft as spring wind that's come from birchen bowers.
Green come the shoots, aye April in the branches,
As winter's wound with her sleight hand she staunches,
Hath of the trees a likeness of the savour:
As white their bark, so white this lady's hours.

CHRISTINA ROSSETTI

A Birthday

My heart is like a singing bird
  Whose nest is in a watered shoot;
My heart is like an apple-tree
  Whose boughs are bent with thickset fruit;
My heart is like a rainbow shell
  That paddles in a halcyon sea;
My heart is gladder than all these
  Because my love is come to me.

Raise me a dais of silk and down;
  Hang it with vair and purple dyes;
Carve it in doves and pomegranates,
  And peacocks with a hundred eyes;
Work it in gold and silver grapes,
  In leaves and silver fleurs-de-lys;
Because the birthday of my life
  Is come, my love is come to me.

Sonnet XXIX

I think of thee! — my thoughts do twine and bud
About thee, as wild vines, about a tree,
Put out broad leaves, and soon there's naught to see
Except the straggling green which hides the wood.
Yet, O my palm-tree, be it understood
I will not have my thoughts instead of thee
Who art dearer, better! Rather, instantly
Renew thy presence; as a strong tree should,
Rustle thy boughs and set thy trunk all bare,
And let these bands of greenery which insphere thee
Drop heavily down — burst, shattered, everywhere!
Because, in this deep joy to see and hear thee
And breathe within thy shadow a new air,
I do not think of thee — I am too near thee.

EDNA ST. VINCENT MILLAY

Love Is Not All

Love is not all: it is not meat nor drink
Nor slumber nor a roof against the rain;
Nor yet a floating spar to men that sink
And rise and sink and rise and sink again;
Love can not fill the thickened lung with breath,
Nor clean the blood, nor set the fractured bone;
Yet many a man is making friends with death
Even as I speak, for lack of love alone.
It well may be that in a difficult hour,
Pinned down by pain and moaning for release,
Or nagged by want past resolution's power,
I might be driven to sell your love for peace,
Or trade the memory of this night for food.
It well may be. I do not think I would.

Robert Browning

Meeting at Night

I

The grey sea and the long black land;
And the yellow half-moon large and low;
And the startled little waves that leap
In fiery ringlets from their sleep,
As I gain the cove with pushing prow,
And quench its speed i' the slushy sand.

II

Then a mile of warm sea-scented beach;
Three fields to cross till a farm appears;
A tap at the pane, the quick sharp scratch
And blue spurt of a lighted match,
And a voice less loud, thro' its joys and fears,
Than the two hearts beating each to each!

PAUL SIMON

The Dangling Conversation

It's a still life water color,
of a now late afternoon,
As the sun shines through the curtained lace
and shadows wash the room.
And we sit and drink our coffee
we are couched in our indifference,
like shells upon the shore
You can hear the ocean roar
in the dangling conversation
and the superficial sighs
the borders of our lives.

And you read your Em'ly Dickinson,
and I my Robert Frost,
And we note our place with book markers
that measure what we've lost.
Like a poem poorly written
we are verses out of rhythm,
couplets out of rhyme,
in syncopated time
and the dangling conversation
and the superficial sighs
are the borders of our lives.

Yes, we speak of things that matter,
with words that must be said,
'Can analysis be worthwhile?'
'Is the theater really dead?'
Now the room is softly faded
and I only kiss your shadow,

I cannot feel your hand,
you're a stranger now unto me
lost in the dangling conversation
and the superficial sighs
in the borders of our lives.

ANONYMOUS

Barbra Allen

In London City where I once did dwell, there's where I got my
  learning,
I fell in love with a pretty young girl, her name was Barbra Allen.
I courted her for seven long years, she said she would not have me;
Then straightway home as I could go and liken to a dying.

I wrote her a letter on my death bed, I wrote it slow and moving;
"Go take this letter to my old true love and tell her I am dying."
She took the letter in her lily-white hand, she read it slow and moving;
"Go take this letter back to him, and tell him I am coming."

As she passed by his dying bed she saw his pale lips quivering;
"No better, no better I'll ever be until I get Barbra Allen."
As she passed by his dying bed; "You're very sick and almost dying,
No better, no better you will ever be, for you can't get Barbra Allen."

As she went down the long stair steps she heard the death bell toning,
And every bell appeared to say, "Hard-hearted Barbra Allen!"
As she went down the long piney walk she heard some small birds
  singing,
And every bird appeared to say, "Hard-hearted Barbra Allen!"

She looked to the East, she looked to the West, she saw the pale corpse
  coming
"Go bring them pale corpse unto me, and let me gaze upon them.
Oh, mama, mama, go make my bed, go make it soft and narrow!
Sweet Willie died today for me, I'll die for him tomorrow!"

They buried Sweet Willie in the old church yard, they buried Miss
  Barbra beside him;

And out of his grave there sprang a red rose, and out of hers a briar.
They grew to the top of the old church tower, they could not grow
   any higher,
They hooked, they tied in a true love's knot, red rose around the briar.

Michael Drayton

Sonnet L

As in some countries far removed from hence
The wretched creature destinèd to die,
Having the judgment due to his offense,
By surgeons begged, their art on him to try;
Which on the living work without remorse,
First make incision on each mastering vein,
Then staunch the bleeding, then trans-pierce the corse,
And with their balms recure the wounds again;
Then poison, and with physic him restore;
Not that they fear the hopeless man to kill,
But their experience to increase the more;
Even so my mistress works upon my ill
    By curing me and killing me each hour
    Only to show her beauty's sovereign power.

OLIVER GOLDSMITH

Woman

When lovely woman stoops to folly,
  And finds too late that men betray,
What charm can soothe her melancholy?
  What art can wash her tears away?

The only art her guilt to cover,
  To hide her shame from ev'ry eye,
To give repentance to her lover,
  And wring his bosom is — to die.

Sir Thomas Wyatt, the Elder

They Flee from Me

They flee from me, that sometime did me seek
　With naked foot, stalking in my chamber.
I have seen them gentle, tame, and meek,
　　That now are wild, and do not remember
　　That sometime they put themselves in danger
　　　To take bread at my hand; and now they range
　　　Busily seeking with a continual change.

Thanked be fortune it hath been otherwise
　Twenty times better; but once, in special,
In thin array, after a pleasant guise,
　　When her loose gown from her shoulders did fall,
　　And she me caught in her arms long and small,
　　　Therewith all sweetly did me kiss
　　　And softly said, 'Dear heart how like you this?'

It was no dream; I lay broad waking:
　But all is turned, thorough my gentleness,
Into a strange fashion of forsaking;
　　And I have leave to go of her goodness,
　　And she also to use newfangleness.
　　　But since that I so kindly am served,
　　　I would fain know what she hath deserved.

Robert Graves

Spoils

When all is over and you march for home,
The spoils of war are easily disposed of:
Standards, weapons of combat, helmets, drums
May decorate a staircase or a study,
While lesser gleanings of the battlefield —
Coins, watches, wedding-rings, gold teeth and such —
Are sold anonymously for solid cash.

The spoils of love present a different case,
When all is over and you march for home:
That lock of hair, these letters and the portrait
May not be publicly displayed; nor sold;
Nor burned; nor returned (the heart being obstinate) —
Yet never dare entrust them to a safe
For fear they burn a hole through two-foot steel.

ROBERT HERRICK

To the Virgins, to Make Much of Time

Gather ye Rose-buds while ye may,
　　Old Time is still a flying:
And this same flower that smiles to day,
　　To morrow will be dying.

The glorious Lamp of Heaven, the Sun,
　　The higher he's a getting;
The sooner will his Race be run,
　　And neerer he's to Setting.

That Age is best, which is the first,
　　When Youth and Blood are warmer;
But being spent, the worse, and worst
　　Times, still succeed the former.

Then be not coy, but use your time;
　　And while ye may, goe marry:
For having lost but once your prime,
　　You may for ever tarry.

EDMUND WALLER

Goe Lovely Rose

Goe lovely Rose,
    Tell her that wastes her time and me,
    That now she knowes,
When I resemble her to thee,
    How sweet and fair she seems to be.

    Tell her that's young,
And shuns to have her graces spied,
    That hadst thou sprung
In deserts where no men abide,
    Thou must have uncommended died.

    Small is the worth
Of beauty from the light retir'd:
    Bid her come forth,
Suffer her selfe to be desir'd,
    And not blush so to be admir'd.

    Then die, that she
The common fate of all things rare
    May read in thee,
How small a part of time they share,
    That are so wondrous sweet and faire.

SAMUEL DANIEL

Sonnet XXXIII

When men shall find thy flower, thy glory, pass,
   And thou with careful brow sitting alone
Received hast this message from thy glass,
   That tells the truth and says that all is gone,
Fresh shalt thou see in me the wounds thou madest,
   Though spent thy flame, in me the heat remaining;
I that have loved thee thus before thou fadest,
   My faith shall wax, when thou art in thy waning.
The world shall find this miracle in me,
   That fire can burn when all the matter's spent;
Then what my faith hath been thyself shalt see,
   And that thou wast unkind thou mayst repent.
     Thou mayst repent that thou hast scorned my tears,
     When winter snows upon thy sable hairs.

GEORGE MEREDITH

Modern Love

By this he knew she wept with waking eyes:
That, at his hand's light quiver by her head,
The strange low sobs that shook their common bed
Were called into her with a sharp surprise,
And strangled mute, like little gaping snakes,
Dreadfully venomous to him. She lay
Stone-still, and the long darkness flowed away
With muffled pulses. Then, as midnight makes
Her giant heart of Memory and Tears
Drink the pale drug of silence, and so beat
Sleep's heavy measure, they from head to feet
Were moveless, looking through their dead black years,
By vain regret scrawled over the blank wall.
Like sculptured effigies they might be seen
Upon their marriage-tomb, the sword between;
Each wishing for the sword that severs all.

William Shakespeare

Sonnet LXXIII

That time of year thou mayst in me behold
When yellow leaves, or none, or few, do hang
Upon those boughs which shake against the cold,
Bare ruined choirs, where late the sweet birds sang.
In me thou see'st the twilight of such day
As after sunset fadeth in the west;
Which by and by black night doth take away,
Death's second self that seals up all in rest.
In me thou see'st the glowing of such fire,
That on the ashes of his youth doth lie,
As the deathbed whereon it must expire,
Consumed with that which it was nourished by.
This thou perceiv'st, which makes thy love more strong,
To love that well which thou must leave ere long.

William Cullen Bryant

To the Fringed Gentian

Thou blossom bright with autumn dew,
And colored with the heaven's own blue,
That openest when the quiet light
Succeeds the keen and frosty night —

Thou comest not when violets lean
O'er wandering brooks and springs unseen,
Or columbines, in purple dressed,
Nod o'er the ground-bird's hidden nest.

Thou waitest late and com'st alone,
When woods are bare and birds are flown,
And frosts and shortening days portend
The aged year is near his end.

Then doth thy sweet and quiet eye
Look through its fringes to the sky,
Blue — blue — as if that sky let fall
A flower from its cerulean wall.

I would that thus, when I shall see
The hour of death draw near to me,
Hope, blossoming within my heart,
May look to heaven as I depart.

John Donne

Holy Sonnet X

Death, be not proud, though some have calléd thee
Mighty and dreadful, for thou art not so;
For those whom thou think'st thou dost overthrow
Die not, poor Death, nor yet canst thou kill me.
From rest and sleep, which but thy pictures be,
Much pleasure; then from thee much more must flow,
And soonest our best men with thee do go,
Rest of their bones, and soul's delivery.
Thou art slave to fate, chance, kings, and desperate men,
And dost with poison, war, and sickness dwell,
And poppy or charms can make us sleep as well
And better than thy stroke; why swell'st thou then?
One short sleep past, we wake eternally
And death shall be no more; Death, thou shalt die.

Henry Wadsworth Longfellow

Mezzo Cammin

Written at Boppard on the Rhine August 25, 1842,
Just before Leaving for Home

Half of my life is gone, and I have let
    The years slip from me and have not fulfilled
    The aspiration of my youth, to build
    Some tower of song with lofty parapet.
Not indolence, nor pleasure, nor the fret
    Of restless passions that would not be stilled,
    But sorrow, and a care that almost killed,
    Kept me from what I may accomplish yet;
Though, half-way up the hill, I see the Past
    Lying beneath me with its sounds and sights, —
    A city in the twilight dim and vast,
With smoking roofs, soft bells, and gleaming lights, —
    And hear above me on the autumnal blast
The cataract of Death far thundering from the heights.

Thomas Gray

Elegy Written in a
Country Church-yard

The Curfew tolls the knell of parting day,
The lowing herd wind slowly o'er the lea,
The plowman homeward plods his weary way,
And leaves the world to darkness and to me.

Now fades the glimmering landscape on the sight,
And all the air a solemn stillness holds,
Save where the beetle wheels his droning flight,
And drowsy tinklings lull the distant folds;

Save that from yonder ivy-mantled tow'r
The mopeing owl does to the moon complain
Of such, as wand'ring near her secret bow'r,
Molest her ancient solitary reign.

Beneath those rugged elms, that yew-tree's shade,
Where heaves the turf in many a mould'ring heap,
Each in his narrow cell for ever laid,
The rude Forefathers of the hamlet sleep.

The breezy call of incense-breathing Morn,
The swallow twitt'ring from the straw-built shed,
The cock's shrill clarion, or the echoing horn,
No more shall rouse them from their lowly bed.

For them no more the blazing hearth shall burn,
Or busy housewife ply her evening care:
No children run to lisp their sire's return,
Or climb his knees the envied kiss to share.

Oft did the harvest to their sickle yield,
Their furrow oft the stubborn glebe has broke;
How jocund did they drive their team afield!
How bow'd the woods beneath their sturdy stroke!

Let not Ambition mock their useful toil,
Their homely joys, and destiny obscure;
Nor Grandeur hear with a disdainful smile,
The short and simple annals of the poor.

The boast of heraldry, the pomp of pow'r,
And all that beauty, all that wealth e'er gave,
Awaits alike th' inevitable hour.
The paths of glory lead but to the grave.

Nor you, ye Proud, impute to These the fault,
If Mem'ry o'er their Tomb no Trophies raise,
Where thro' the long-drawn isle and fretted vault
The pealing anthem swells the note of praise.

Can storied urn or animated bust
Back to its mansion call the fleeting breath?
Can Honour's voice provoke the silent dust,
Or Flatt'ry sooth the dull cold ear of Death?

Perhaps in this neglected spot is laid
Some heart once pregnant with celestial fire;
Hands, that the rod of empire might have sway'd,
Or wak'd to extasy the living lyre.

But Knowledge to their eyes her ample page
Rich with the spoils of time did ne'er unroll;
Chill Penury repress'd their noble rage,
And froze the genial current of the soul.

Full many a gem of purest ray serene,
The dark unfathom'd caves of ocean bear:
Full many a flower is born to blush unseen,
And waste its sweetness on the desert air.

Some village-Hampden, that with dauntless breast
The little Tyrant of his fields withstood;
Some mute inglorious Milton here may rest,
Some Cromwell guiltless of his country's blood.

Th' applause of list'ning senates to command,
The threats of pain and ruin to despise,
To scatter plenty o'er a smiling land,
And read their hist'ry in a nation's eyes,

Their lot forbad: nor circumscrib'd alone
Their growing virtues, but their crimes confin'd;
Forbad to wade through slaughter to a throne,
And shut the gates of mercy on mankind,

The struggling pangs of conscious truth to hide,
To quench the blushes of ingenuous shame,
Or heap the shrine of Luxury and Pride
With incense kindled at the Muse's flame.

Far from the madding crowd's ignoble strife,
Their sober wishes never learn'd to stray;
Along the cool sequester'd vale of life
They kept the noiseless tenor of their way.

Yet ev'n these bones from insult to protect
Some frail memorial still erected nigh,
With uncouth rhimes and shapeless sculpture deck'd,
Implores the passing tribute of a sigh.

185

Their name, their years, spelt by th' unletter'd muse,
The place of fame and elegy supply:
And many a holy text around she strews,
That teach the rustic moralist to die.

For who to dumb Forgetfulness a prey,
This pleasing anxious being e'er resign'd,
Left the warm precincts of the chearful day,
Nor cast one longing ling'ring look behind?

On some fond breast the parting soul relies,
Some pious drops the closing eye requires;
Ev'n from the tomb the voice of Nature cries,
Ev'n in our Ashes live their wonted Fires.

For thee, who mindful of th' unhonour'd Dead
Dost in these lines their artless tale relate;
If chance, by lonely contemplation led,
Some kindred Spirit shall inquire thy fate,

Haply some hoary-headed Swain may say,
'Oft have we seen him at the peep of dawn
'Brushing with hasty steps the dews away
'To meet the sun upon the upland lawn.

'There at the foot of yonder nodding beech
'That wreathes its old fantastic roots so high,
'His listless length at noontide would he stretch,
'And pore upon the brook that babbles by.

'Hard by yon wood, now smiling as in scorn,
'Mutt'ring his wayward fancies he would rove,
'Now drooping, woeful wan, like one forlorn,
'Or craz'd with care, or cross'd in hopeless love.

'One morn I miss'd him on the custom'd hill,
'Along the heath and near his fav'rite tree;
'Another came; nor yet beside the rill,
'Nor up the lawn, nor at the wood was he;

'The next with dirges due in sad array
'Slow thro' the church-way path we saw him born.
'Approach and read (for thou can'st read) the lay,
'Grav'd on the stone beneath yon aged thorn.'

The Epitaph

Here rests his head upon the lap of Earth
A Youth to Fortune and to Fame unknown.
Fair Science frown'd not on his humble birth,
And Melancholy mark'd him for her own.

Large was his bounty, and his soul sincere,
Heav'n did a recompence as largely send:
He gave to Mis'ry all he had, a tear,
He gain'd from Heav'n ('twas all he wish'd) a friend.

No farther seek his merits to disclose,
Or draw his frailties from their dread abode,
(There they alike in trembling hope repose,)
The bosom of his Father and his God.

John Webster

The Shrouding of the Duchess of Malfi

Hark! Now everything is still,
The screech-owl and the whistler shrill,
Call upon our dame aloud,
And bid her quickly don her shroud!

Much you had of land and rent;
Your length in clay's now competent:
A long war disturb'd your mind;
Here your perfect peace is sign'd.

Of what is 't fools make such vain keeping?
Sin their conception, their birth weeping,
Their life a general mist of error,
Their death a hideous storm of terror.
Strew your hair with powders sweet,
Don clean linen, bathe your feet,
And — the foul fiend more to check —
A crucifix let bless your neck:
'Tis now full tide 'tween night and day;
End your groan and come away.

John Keats

Ode on a Grecian Urn

I

Thou still unravish'd bride of quietness,
  Thou foster-child of silence and slow time,
Sylvan historian, who canst thus express
  A flowery tale more sweetly than our rhyme:
What leaf-fring'd legend haunts about thy shape
  Of deities or mortals, or of both,
    In Tempe or the dales of Arcady?
  What men or gods are these? What maidens loth?
What mad pursuit? What struggle to escape?
    What pipes and timbrels? What wild ecstasy?

II

Heard melodies are sweet, but those unheard
  Are sweeter; therefore, ye soft pipes, play on;
Not to the sensual ear, but, more endear'd,
  Pipe to the spirit ditties of no tone:
Fair youth, beneath the trees, thou canst not leave
  Thy song, nor ever can those trees be bare;
    Bold Lover, never, never canst thou kiss,
Though winning near the goal — yet, do not grieve;
  She cannot fade, though thou hast not thy bliss,
    For ever wilt thou love, and she be fair!

III

Ah, happy, happy boughs! that cannot shed
  Your leaves, nor ever bid the Spring adieu;
And, happy melodist, unwearied,
  For ever piping songs for ever new;

More happy love! more happy, happy love!
    For ever warm and still to be enjoy'd,
        For ever panting, and for ever young;
All breathing human passion far above,
    That leaves a heart high-sorrowful and cloy'd,
        A burning forehead, and a parching tongue.

IV

Who are these coming to the sacrifice?
    To what green altar, O mysterious priest,
Lead'st thou that heifer lowing at the skies,
    And all her silken flanks with garlands drest?
What little town by river or sea shore,
    Or mountain-built with peaceful citadel,
        Is emptied of this folk, this pious morn?
And, little town, thy streets for evermore
    Will silent be; and not a soul to tell
        Why thou art desolate, can e'er return.

V

O Attic shape! Fair attitude! with brede
    Of marble men and maidens overwrought,
With forest branches and the trodden weed;
    Thou, silent form, dost tease us out of thought
As doth eternity: Cold Pastoral!
    When old age shall this generation waste,
        Thou shalt remain, in midst of other woe
Than ours, a friend to man, to whom thou say'st,
    'Beauty is truth, truth beauty,' — that is all
        Ye know on earth, and all ye need to know.

ROBINSON JEFFERS

The Deer Lay Down Their Bones

I followed the narrow cliffside trail half way up the mountain
Above the deep river-canyon. There was a little cataract crossed the
  path, flinging itself
Over tree roots and rocks, shaking the jeweled fern-fronds, bright
  bubbling water
Pure from the mountain, but a bad smell came up. Wondering at
  it I clambered down the steep stream
Some forty feet, and found in the midst of bush-oak and laurel,
Hung like a bird's nest on the precipice brink a small hidden clearing,
Grass and a shallow pool. But all about there were bones lying in
  the grass, clean bones and stinking bones,
Antlers and bones: I understood that the place was a refuge for
  wounded deer; there are so many
Hurt ones escape the hunters and limp away to lie hidden; here they
  have water for the awful thirst
And peace to die in; dense green laurel and grim cliff
Make sanctuary, and a sweet wind blows upward from the deep
  gorge. — I wish my bones were with theirs.
But that's a foolish thing to confess, and a little cowardly. We know
  that life
Is on the whole quite equally good and bad, mostly gray neutral, and
  can be endured
To the dim end, no matter what magic of grass, water and precipice,
  and pain of wounds,
Makes death look dear. We have been given life and have used
  it — not a great gift perhaps — but in honesty
Should use it all. Mine's empty since my love died — Empty? The
  flame-haired grandchild with great blue eyes
That look like hers? — What can I do for the child? I gaze at her and
  wonder what sort of man

In the fall of the world . . . I am growing old, that is the trouble. My
  children and little grandchildren
Will find their way, and why should I wait ten years yet, having lived
  sixty-seven, ten years more or less,
Before I crawl out on a ledge of rock and die snapping, like a wolf
Who has lost his mate? — I am bound by my own thirty-year-old
  decision: who drinks the wine
Should take the dregs; even in the bitter lees and sediment
New discovery may lie. The deer in that beautiful place lay down
  their bones: I must wear mine.

WILFRED OWEN

Anthem for Doomed Youth

What passing-bells for these who die as cattle?
  Only the monstrous anger of the guns.
  Only the stuttering rifles' rapid rattle
Can patter out their hasty orisons.
No mockeries for them; no prayers nor bells,
Nor any voice of mourning save the choirs, —
The shrill, demented choirs of wailing shells;
And bugles calling for them from sad shires.

What candles may be held to speed them all?
  Not in the hands of boys, but in their eyes
Shall shine the holy glimmers of good-byes.
  The pallor of girls' brows shall be their pall;
Their flowers the tenderness of patient minds,
And each slow dusk a drawing-down of blinds.

JOHN SCOTT OF AMWELL

Retort on the Foregoing

I hate that drum's discordant sound,
Parading round, and round, and round:
To thoughtless youth it pleasure yields,
And lures from cities and from fields,
To sell their liberty for charms
Of tawdry lace, and glittering arms;
And when Ambition's voice commands,
To march, and fight, and fall, in foreign lands.

I hate that drum's discordant sound,
Parading round, and round, and round:
To me it talks of ravag'd plains,
And burning towns, and ruin'd swains,
And mangled limbs, and dying groans,
And widows' tears, and orphans' moans;
And all that Misery's hand bestows,
To fill the catalogue of human woes.

A. E. HOUSMAN

To an Athlete Dying Young

The time you won your town the race
We chaired you through the market-place;
Man and boy stood cheering by,
And home we brought you shoulder-high.

To-day, the road all runners come,
Shoulder-high we bring you home,
And set you at your threshold down,
Townsman of a stiller town.

Smart lad, to slip betimes away
From fields where glory does not stay
And early though the laurel grows
It withers quicker than the rose.

Eyes the shady night has shut
Cannot see the record cut,
And silence sounds no worse than cheers
After earth has stopped the ears:

Now you will not swell the rout
Of lads that wore their honours out,
Runners whom renown outran
And the name died before the man.

So set, before its echoes fade,
The fleet foot on the sill of shade,
And hold to the low lintel up
The still-defended challenge-cup.

And round that early-laurelled head
Will flock to gaze the strengthless dead,
And find unwithered on its curls
The garland briefer than a girl's.

KARL SHAPIRO

Auto Wreck

Its quick soft silver bell beating, beating,
And down the dark one ruby flare
Pulsing out red light like an artery,
The ambulance at top speed floating down
Past beacons and illuminated clocks
Wings in a heavy curve, dips down,
And brakes speed, entering the crowd.
The doors leap open, emptying light;
Stretchers are laid out, the mangled lifted
And stowed into the little hospital.
Then the bell, breaking the hush, tolls once,
And the ambulance with its terrible cargo
Rocking, slightly rocking, moves away,
As the doors, an afterthought, are closed.

We are deranged, walking among the cops
Who sweep glass and are large and composed.
One is still making notes under the light.
One with a bucket douches pounds of blood
Into the street and gutter.
One hangs lanterns on the wrecks that cling,
Empty husks of locusts, to iron poles.

Our throats were tight as tourniquets,
Our feet were bound with splints, but now,
Like convalescents intimate and gauche,
We speak through sickly smiles and warn
With the stubborn saw of common sense,
The grim joke and the banal resolution.
The traffic moves around with care,

But we remain, touching a wound
That opens to our richest horror.
Already old, the question Who shall die?
Becomes unspoken Who is innocent?
For death in war is done by hands;
Suicide has cause and stillbirth, logic;
And cancer, simple as a flower, blooms.
But this invites the occult mind,
Cancels our physics with a sneer,
And spatters all we knew of denouement
Across the expedient and wicked stones.

Randall Jarrell

The Death of the Ball Turret Gunner

From my mother's sleep I fell into the State,
And I hunched in its belly till my wet fur froze.
Six miles from earth, loosed from its dream of life,
I woke to black flak and the nightmare fighters.
When I died they washed me out of the turret with a hose.

W. B. YEATS

The Second Coming

Turning and turning in the widening gyre
The falcon cannot hear the falconer;
Things fall apart; the centre cannot hold;
Mere anarchy is loosed upon the world,
The blood-dimmed tide is loosed, and everywhere
The ceremony of innocence is drowned;
The best lack all conviction, while the worst
Are full of passionate intensity.

Surely some revelation is at hand;
Surely the Second Coming is at hand.
The Second Coming! Hardly are those words out
When a vast image out of *Spiritus Mundi*
Troubles my sight: somewhere in sands of the desert
A shape with lion body and the head of a man,
A gaze blank and pitiless as the sun,
Is moving its slow thighs, while all about it
Reel shadows of the indignant desert birds.
The darkness drops again; but now I know
That twenty centuries of stony sleep
Were vexed to nightmare by a rocking cradle,
And what rough beast, its hour come round at last,
Slouches towards Bethlehem to be born?